W9-CIN-115

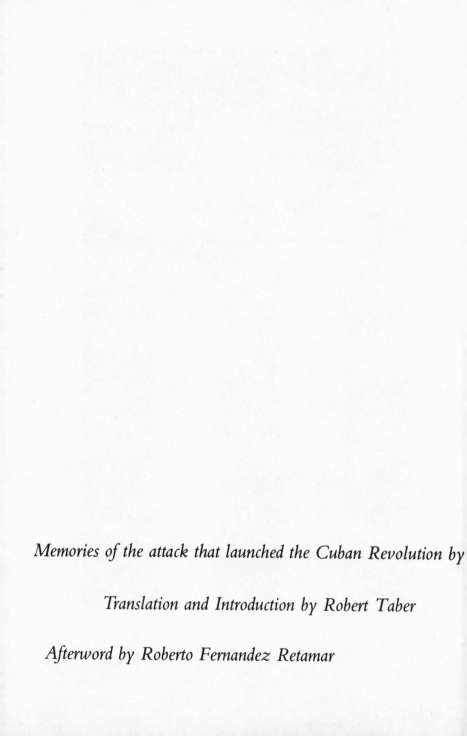

Memories of the attack that launched the Cuban Revolution by

Translation and Introduction by Robert Taber

Afterword by Roberto Fernandez Retamar

MONCADA

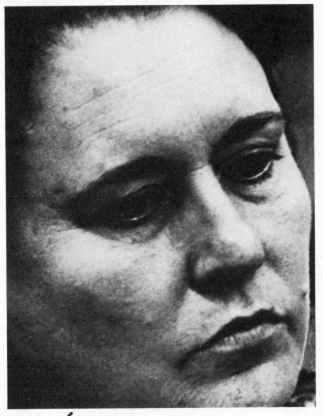

HAYDÉE SANTAMARÍA

LYLE STUART INC.   *Secaucus, N.J.*

Library of Congress Cataloging in Publication Data
Santamaría, Haydée.
   Moncada, memories of the attack that launched
the Cuban Revolution.

    1. Cuba—History—Moncada Barracks Attack,
1953—Personal narratives. 2. Cuba—History—
Revolution, 1959—Personal narratives.
3. Santamaría, Haydée. 4. Revolutionists—Cuba—
Biography. 5. Castro, Fidel, 1927–
I. Title.
F1787.5.S23   972.91′063   79-23960
ISBN 0-8184-0278-4

CONTENTS

INTRODUCTION

☆

HAYDÉE SANTAMARÍA is one of the great names of the Cuban Revolution. Circumstance, talent, and natural inclination have made her a cultural rather than a political force; she is known in the hemisphere today as head of Casa de las Américas, the Latin American and Caribbean arts institute that she founded in 1959. But revolutionary history casts her in another light: Cubans know her as a legendary underground fighter, an original member of the tiny *fidelista* inner circle that plotted the downfall of the dictator, Fulgencio Batista, from the day that Batista, pistol in hand, seized power in Havana on March 10, 1952.

A sensitive, rather shy young countrywoman, born and raised on a sugar plantation, Santamaría became organizer, instigator, fund raiser, terrorist tactician, and for a time national coordinator of the Cuban underground that supported Fidel Castro during his long guerrilla war in the mountains of the Sierra Maestra, from the improbable, disastrous landing of 1956 to the incredible triumph of the first day of 1959.

Her revolutionary credentials were authenticated long before that day arrived. Her blood baptism came on July 26, 1953, name date of the *Movimiento Revolucionario 26 de julio,* when Castro mounted his first armed challenge to Batista, the ill-starred assault on the yellow-walled fortress called Cuartel Moncada, in Santiago de Cuba, province of Oriente.

Haydée was one of two women to take part in the Santiago uprising. Before another sunrise, she had lost a beloved brother and a fiancé, both murdered in the interrogation cells of Moncada. In the reprisals of the following days, some seventy of her comrades died in summary wayside executions or under torture in the barracks.

Subsequent developments produced the capture of Fidel Castro, the safe surrender of remnants of the assault force under the mediation of the archbishop of Santiago, Fidel's secret trial, and the mass trial of 122 of his alleged co-conspirators. Most of these, as Haydée notes, were innocent of any connection with the assault; at worst they were Castro sympathizers, rounded up by Baptista's notorious military intelligence service (SIM) as substitutes for murdered captives lying in unmarked graves.

The national scandal of the post-Moncada blood bath forced some discreet acquittals and some nominal sentences. What just penalty could be imposed on defendants who were, in truth, victims? How punish a young woman who had been forced to listen to the screams of her dying brother as soldiers gouged out his eyes?

Haydée Santamaría and the young woman attorney Melba Hernandez were sentenced to six months in the penitentiary at Guanajay. Both had been captured in the civic hospital near the fortress, attending the wounded.

Where were their missing companions?

"I left the hospital with twenty-five[1] comrades," Haydée told the court. "You symbols of justice, tell me where they are."

---

[1] In fact, twenty-one, including Abel Santamaría, Fidel's second-in-command.

The three judges were silent. Of the rebel group at the hospital, only the two women had survived.

Fidel, tried separately, was sentenced to fifteen years in the military prison on the Isle of Pines; his brother, Raúl to thirteen years. But rising political pressures in Havana were soon to produce a general amnesty, reluctantly granted by Batista. On May 15, 1955, the surviving leaders of the Moncada attack were released.

Haydée was on hand to embrace them—and soon after to wish them godspeed as they sailed into exile in Mexico, to prepare the pocket invasion that opened the guerrilla war in the Sierra.

The foregoing brief chronology has been offered as a factual framework for Haydée Santamaría's personal recollections, drawn from a long, informal discussion before an audience of students in the School of Political Science of the University of Havana.[2]

[2]July 13, 1967

Her recollections assume, correctly as regards a Cuban audience, familiarity with the persons, places, and political context of the Moncada assault. Haydée, for her part, is preoccupied not with details but with significance. Her effort is to find personal meaning in an historic event that was, for her, an overwhelming, traumatic, transforming experience.

Santamaría has spoken little of Moncada, and never before in public. Her recollections are hesitant, tentative: there is so much to be told, but how best to tell it, where to begin? As the event recedes in time, she says, and its consequences unfold on an ever-wider historical screen, it becomes increasingly harder for her to discuss the acts and circumstances of that bloody twenty-sixth of July—so near, so remote, so fatefully past.

One finds in her groping, too, something of the strange amnesia of the survivor for whom the shocks of battle have been too great, flooding the senses, disordering the sequential, recording mind, so that what remains are scraps of brilliant but often inconsequential detail, tattered by the torrent of ineffable, unreconciled emotion that is the indelible true content of the experience.

Who was the village girl who went to Moncada? What is she now? Her own words reveal her.

She has fought and killed. She grieves for those who have fallen—on either side. "I can tell you," she says, "that it moved me to see even an enemy fall, to see him die. . . . When I saw his body fall, it disturbed me so much that for a long time I could not forget his falling."

Her political convictions are empirical; they arise from a sense of the Cuban imperative. At a certain juncture, she says, she saw that it was not enough to exchange one political figure for another; it became necessary to change systems in order to change men.

She has an impatience that amounts to contempt for the cold bones of formal law, for political arrangements that seem to her to fall short of the fully and naturally human. "For me," she says, "to be a Communist does not mean only joining a party; it means having an attitude towards life."

In the context, a personal recollection of one's own may be permitted. It happened that in early April 1957 the writer accompanied Haydée Santamaría on a journey into the Sierra Maestra. My purpose was to film an interview with Fidel, soon after his landing from Mexico. Hers was to deliver funds collected from sympathizers in Havana and to confer on organization and strategy.

The motor trip down the length of the central highway from the capital to Manzanillo in Oriente, staging point for the march into the Sierra, took two days and nights. It was perilous for Haydée, whose name and face were well known to police and to the *pistoleros* of Batista's SIM; and it was the more dangerous because it followed by only a few weeks an abortive attack on the presidential palace, aimed at Batista himself. Five members of the palace guard and thirty-five assailants had been killed; reprisals brought the toll close to eighty.

Haydée's eyes were red and swollen when we met, and she was sniffling; a cold, she said; but she brightened up and chatted amiably as the trip proceeded, after some obscure talk, passing over my head, about bus schedules and a missed appointment.

In the middle of the journey, she suddenly asked me to "hold something," and thrust a big bundle of currency at me, some three thousand pesos in small bills. We were going to risk a Sunday dinner in a restaurant, and she said she thought that, should we be arrested, I would have a better chance than she to keep the money; as a journalist I could say that it was expense money.

When I returned it at the end of the trip, she counted it, frowning, and asked, "Are you sure it's all there?"

I patted my pockets and said, yes, I was perfectly sure.

Counting again, she muttered, "I'm sure there was more." Then, looking up and seeing my expression, she burst into laughter. It was her little joke; at the same time, it was a test: she was not at all sure that she trusted any *gringo* reporter.

In Manzanillo, she told another member of the movement that I might, after all, be honest, but asked: "Why wouldn't he talk to me?"

An explanation would have been simple enough: I did not know who she was; I had scarcely heard of Moncada. Half the time I had not understood what she was saying; my spoken Spanish was barbarous at best. Nor was I aware, until long afterwards, that at the time of our departure from Havana it was feared that her husband, Armando Hart,[3] had been arrested in the continuing roundup that followed the palace attack. He had planned to go to the Sierra with us; it was he who had missed the appointment at the bus station.

Was he alive or dead? Behind bars or still free? Haydée's face never betrayed her fears, neither on the cross-country journey nor later in the Sierra. She had, as she has remarked, "an attitude towards life." She accepted its risks, finding no alternative but to go forward.

Robert Taber
July, 1979

[3]Now Cuban Minister of Culture

MONCADA

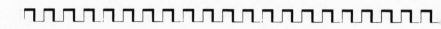

I

☆

**"TO BUY RIFLES,
TO BUY BULLETS,
WE HAD TO STOP EATING"**

*Revolutionary conspiracy was scarcely a novelty in
Cuba when Fidel Castro sounded his* grito de Mon-
cada *of July 26, 1953, his incendiary call to arms.
Nor was rifle rule the innovation of General
Fulgencio Batista. Both were rooted in the Republic
from its inception.*

*Politics was a struggle for spoils; the bomb and the
bullet were ballots. Secret societies proliferated. Students were revolutionaries almost by definition: the
fathers of the youths who battled Batista had fought
against the Machado dictatorship in their time.*

*Batista, strongman of the Sergeants' Revolt of
1933, had ruled de facto for the greater part of twenty
years, answering opposition with assassination,
breaking strikes with machinegun fire as the good
steward of sugar barons, banks, gambling syndicates,
and the great corporate interests of the North. When*

he again reached for the pistol, aborted an election, and deposed an incumbent president in his military golpe of March 10, 1952, he was merely affirming an established pattern.

His opponents, too, were figures in the same static tapestry: disappointed candidates (Fidel was one), political parties eager for "civic dialogue" and profitable compromise, idealistic youths of radical disposition, armed with the rusty weapons of their predecessors and ready to die—but under whose leadership, and to what end? The stage had long been set. March 10 was the curtain-raiser, the signal for a new beginning. It is at this point that Haydée Santamaría takes up her story.

LIKE MUCH OF THE YOUTH of that time, I believe, we belonged to various distinct political groups. There was, for example, a certain "Triple A." Another group was . . . But I have already forgotten all those letters. It was a tremendous thing. I don't know who used to come, I don't know how many. But on that March 10 we were ready to fight alongside any group, because the most important thing, it seemed to me, was not to accept what had been imposed on us [i.e., the Batista coup d'état]. And this was one way of fighting it, although we may not have been in agreement concerning all that had gone before.

This was our position until we found Fidel.

Finding him, we could begin to speak of a truth and a reality; we could begin with *something*—for we had had nothing.

Everybody was boasting of what they had. Forty thousand airplanes, for all I know! To hear them speak, they had enough arms for a world war. And then we found Fidel, who said: "We have nothing, there is nothing, and the problem now is not one of *how much,* but of beginning."

We started out with some old machine guns that I doubt had ever been fired. So that was something. Then under Fidel's direction we began to collect other weapons, ammunition, some little rifles that we could use for practice. To us, those little rifles were cannon!

What we were going to do was already under discussion, although the precise action was not specified. Fidel taught us that it could only be done if it were kept secret.

To buy rifles, to buy bullets, we had to stop eating. Our comrades had to stop smoking, they had to give up their little three-cent cups of coffee to buy those rifles and all those bullets. But the greatest thing is that we never *felt* hungry.

Seldom in our lives have we been happier than when our small group was getting ready for Moncada. We had no idea what Moncada would be, but it didn't matter, because in any case it would be Moncada. Seldom were we happier than when groups like that, a small one . . . Perhaps right now I'm remembering all those who used to visit us in the apartment Abel [Santamaría] and I shared in 25th Street [in Havana]. Everything was done there; we lived there for days, months, no sad moments, perhaps as we had never lived before. Because afterwards the struggle was greater, the groups were larger, and the battle spread over the whole island.

In spite of being concentrated, holed up in that tiny apartment—because it *was* a tiny apartment—we all had enough room, we all ate, we all lived, and we were all happy. Never have I tasted more delicious meals than those, never have we shared anything the way we shared that little corner.

We would cook for five, and twenty would turn up; and all twenty ate, or at least they thought they were eating, although food for five did not stretch far for twenty; even for five it was too little. But the joy of our being there all together, the joy of sharing everything . . . In that little hole in the wall, we all slept and we all had enough room. The floor seemed the most comfortable, springiest mattress in the world!

That is why I say that it was easy, even if thoughts of family, the thought of their pain and incomprehension—perhaps the hardest part—came to everyone's mind, even knowing where our duty lay and knowing that sooner or later they would understand. Or at least that is what we had to think.

It has always been difficult to go back to that apartment that I remember as so filled with life, because it is pain to realize that there is no life there anymore. Today it is arranged as it was in those days, but there is no life in it! If instead of fixing it up in that way, if there were some life in it, if there were some students, if it were always filled with people, if we could see those same men . . . it would be easy to go back. But it is hard to think there is no life where there was so much.

From that apartment, the various groups set out for Santiago.

II

☆

"THE NIGHT WAS A NIGHT OF LIFE, THE STARS WERE BIGGER AND BRIGHTER"

From Havana, the assault groups traveled by car over the central highway to a farm at Siboney, twenty miles from Santiago, procured as a rallying point and headquarters. One group of twenty-seven was sent to attack the garrison at Bayamo, on the Río Cauto north of Santiago. Like those at Moncada, most of the Bayamo group were to die in the attempt—or to be slaughtered after it.

SOMEONE ASKS ABOUT the night before the attack on Moncada, the night of the 25th of July. If I could put myself there, I could say more. Really, for me it was to be again a girl going to her fifteenth birthday party. It was one of the most joyful of nights. My impressions? Everything stood out, above all the fact that although I could not know what would happen, I knew that it would be something great. I wondered whether I would ever see again the sunshine of my country—for this alone is worth the pain of living. I knew that if I did not see it, that, too, would be great.

The night was a night of life, because we wanted to see, to feel, to look at all that we might never see or feel or look at again. We went out in the patio, and the moon was bigger and more brilliant; the stars were bigger and brighter; the palms taller and greener; the faces of our friends were faces we might never see again but would have with us always.

Everything was more beautiful, everything was larger, lovelier, finer; we felt ourselves to be better, kinder. I was thinking of my little niece and found her the most beautiful little girl in the world, because, perhaps, I might never see her or hold her again.

I looked at my brother Abel and it comforted me to think that if I never saw him again it would be because I, too, no longer lived.

We looked at Fidel, and it was as though

something told us that he would surely live; perhaps he might be the only survivor, because *he* had to live.

We went to Moncada with the same feelings as when we go out to cut sugar cane today. I went with the feelings I have now when I see schools filled with boys and girls from the countryside—for when we went to Moncada we lived all this in our minds. We were not sure that we would live to see it, but we had the certainty of its coming. And so we went in search of life, and not of death.

But of course death was there, shattering and devouring everything. There were moments when there was nothing to be seen or felt but death on every side. We looked for life—and could not find it. There were moments when I could not accept the thought of someone living who ought not to be living, and of another dying who ought to live.

There were also the most luminous moments imaginable, for never have I seen such strong resistance, and with so little for defense.

When you fight under a certain equality of conditions, or with the support of the people, it is one thing, but when you are fighting practically with a stick, and without the support of the people—for they did not know that we were fighting,[1] or why—simply to stand firm is magnificent.

I am not tragic, neither here nor there [at Moncada]. My temperament is rather informal; when I say informal, it is partly a matter of collecting myself. Among my friends I am famous for my inability to conduct a meeting; that is, this sort of formal, analytical meeting. I lack the temperament for it. I am not sad, certainly, not there or here, not before or afterwards.

[1] The Moncada assailants went into battle clad in the identical khaki uniform of the Cuban army. Hearing the shooting, seeing the uniforms, people in Santiago assumed that they were witnessing an army insurrection.

III

☆

**"THE FIGHTING WOULD GO ON
IN THE MOUNTAINS"**

The force assembled at Siboney consisted of 165 fighters, most of them armed only with light sporting pieces, .22-caliber rifles, shotguns. A tragic blunder kept many—at his trial Fidel said perhaps half the force—from reaching the fortress. And a further misadventure, the chance arrival of an army patrol car at Moncada, gave the alarm and aborted the attack. Haydée explains:

THAT NIGHT all of the men were prepared to go into combat. We had been mobilized on many occasions before and had always answered the roll call, assuming that there would be fighting. So on the eve of the Moncada action, all were in the appointed place, just as on other occasions we had gone to other locations, near Havana, or in Pinar del Río.

Fidel told us that this time it would really be a day of combat. The battle would be terribly unequal; we must seek to capture the barracks and overcome the garrison,[1] but, understanding the element of surprise and the chance of failure, we must be prepared for it. If the immediate objective could not be achieved, we were to return to Siboney, pick up the ammunition left in reserve there, and rally to continue the fight. Those who succeeded in finding new weapons were to return with them—or if not, with the arms they carried—and head for the mountains.

The fighting would go on there in the mountains; no one could say how long it would last; surely it would be hard. This, in any event, was the plan. If we succeeded in taking the fortress,

---

[1]Moncada was the base of the Maceo Regiment of some 1,500 troops. During the annual carnival, just ending, no more than 500 were expected to be in their barracks. The immediate objective was the armory and its store of military weapons and ammunition.

guns would be given to the people, and in Santiago they would make as much of a stand as
they could. And when there was no longer any
way of holding out in Santiago with the arms
and ammunition acquired [at Moncada], we
would head for the mountains with the many
people we were sure would be ready to follow
us.

At this point, some of our comrades said that
they had no faith in the plan: it was madness,
they said, and could not succeed. I don't know
what they imagined. Perhaps they were simply
frightened. In any case, they were given a car
and instructed to try to return to Havana, but to
be the last to leave. No one was obliged to take
part in the attack. For reasons that are not sub-
jective, we believe that this group must have
jumped the gun and diverted other cars. One
car was to follow the next: we knew that the car
behind Abel's up to a certain point was bound
for such a place, another for the high court, an-

other for the barracks; the worst that could happen was that someone might make a wrong turn, and that would not have been too serious.

Instead it seems that the car bound for Havana went ahead of the column and detoured when it came to Santiago. This caused the cars following it to leave the right road, creating a fatal situation. Those who might have contributed and were really eager to fight—I am referring to the ones who were sidetracked—kept circling Santiago de Cuba again and again. And many were caught and many were murdered, because of those who had decided not to fight.

It was a frightful thing. No charges were brought againt them; they were released. Perhaps their worst offense had been to move on ahead of the main group.

Those ten . . . but I cannot say how many there were. It was not brought out into the open, because Fidel, with his tremendous understanding, did not wish to hold them up to public scorn. Names were not mentioned much; the action had not been forced on anyone. For even in that crisis Fidel had the same sensibility and human fiber that never left him, even in the face of the most crucial decisions.

One of the things he said then was: "Don't

shoot for pleasure; don't kill for pleasure." And the very quality that led him to say, "Don't kill, don't shoot," also kept him from pressing men who were not ready to fight. He refused to brand them as traitors, considering only that they were not, at that time, ready to go along with the plan.

IV

☆

**"IT MOVED ME
TO SEE EVEN AN ENEMY FALL,
TO SEE HIM DIE"**

To strengthen the assault, two buildings commanding the fortress were seized by armed rebel groups: the Saturnino Lora Civil Hospital and the Palace of Justice. Raúl Castro led a squad of snipers to the roof of the courthouse; Haydée Santamaría and Melba Hernandez went to the hospital as part of a contingent of twenty led by Abel Santamaría. With Dr. Mario Muñoz, revolutionary physician, their task was to care for the wounded. They were still there when, three hours after the attack began, the rebel rearguard at Moncada withdrew and troops at last venturing out of the barracks burst into the hospital. Dr. Muñoz was shot down in the street outside, on the pretext that he was escaping. The others were herded into the fortress. Haydée and Melba were the only survivors of their group in the ordeal that followed.

☆

THE STRUGGLE at the hospital was a tiny one, but very great. It was a struggle in which we had already planned, seeing no way out, to die without a single bullet left in our rifles. When it became apparent that there was no escape and that the main battle was over—we could tell by the sound of the shooting dying away—Abel, who was directing us, made the decision to stay and continue the resistance. He told me: "The longer we keep on fighting here, the more of the others we will be able to save. There is always one fighter who must die without a bullet left in his rifle—if a bullet hasn't gotten him first."

What he said impressed me tremendously.

I was impressed, too, by the nurses who helped us, recognizing, without being told and in spite of the uniforms we wore, that we were not the soldiers of despotism.[1]

---

[1]When further resistance was clearly futile, the nurses tried to save members of the group by dressing them in gowns and otherwise disguising them as patients.

At one point I went over to one of them and asked her why she was helping us.

"Because you are good people," she answered.

"And how do you know we're good?"

"Because you're against Batista."

"And how do you know we're against Batista?"

"Because you're good," she said. And I couldn't budge her from that.

And this impressed me greatly; it told me that it was worthwhile to make all kinds of sacrifices. Because how could a person, a woman who was a student nurse, distinguish the good from the bad unless she had been told? And I felt proud, thinking, "They haven't confused us with the bad ones even though we came disguised as the bad ones."

I can tell you that it moved me to see even an enemy fall, to see him die. I was tremendously upset to see the death of one we had come to fight, so much so that it paralyzed me. For I realized that the man had a mother, maybe a wife and children, and had not been born either good or bad; that we had shot him because a system had made him evil, or perhaps he was not even evil.

I was moved for some time by the first man I saw die—a man who had gone there to fight. When I saw his body fall, it disturbed me so much that for a long time I could not forget his falling.

But I don't mean to imply that all this made me weaken and stop looking and stop seeing them fall. We were not doing it for pleasure; it was a necessity.

I believe it takes a great effort to be violent, to go to war. But one has to be violent and to go to war when there is good reason. And what you cannot lose in the face of it all is sensibility. You must keep the same human qualities you had before you started killing. It is painful to kill, but if it is necessary, you must do it.

When in my undercover work I had to plant a bomb—and sometimes it fell to me to do this; that is, to send some man to plant the bomb—I chose the best man, the most sensitive, the most human, the one who would not let bomb planting become second nature and would not get pleasure from it.

I was often asked: "How is it that you send the best man?" And I would say: "Because I never send anyone I don't believe is good. I always send the man I think will do this as a duty, not as a pleasure."

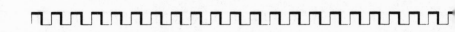

V

☆

"IN A MOMENT I SAW SOME HANDS, SOME FINGERS. I DON'T KNOW HOW I KNEW, BUT— THEY WERE FIDEL'S!"

WHEN MELBA AND I were still in the *cuartel* we had some hope that Fidel was alive, because it was believed that Abel had commanded the assault, and we were sure that if Fidel had died and they had found him there, they would have known at once that he had been the chief.

After two or three days—I don't quite remember how many—they took us to the *vivac*.[1] Melba and I had been kept apart from the others. We did not know how many had been killed—perhaps because we did not want to know. They brought us down from an upper floor of the barracks and took us to a cellar,

[1] *Vicac:* the civil jail or "bivouac," so called because casual prisoners were lodged there for the night.

where we saw a group of comrades. I tried to look at them all at once, to see who was still living. I looked for Fidel, and for Abel and Boris[2]—even knowing that those last two could not be there, I went on looking.[2]

So they took us to the *vivac* and we were there for I don't know how many days. We lost track of time there, the sense of day and night, of life and death. We neither felt nor suffered; we were past knowing what it was to live or die, in a state worse than living or dying.

One day we heard some activity and peeked out. The jail was built around a central courtyard—one would have to know the layout—like some of the homes of Santiago, and the entrance faced the door of our cell. We could only

[2]Boris Luís Santa Coloma, Haydée's fiancé. She knew that neither he nor her brother could be alive, because she had heard their torture and their dying cries, and had been told in her own interrogation what had been done to them.

see through the grating bit by bit: if we wanted to see feet, we had to crouch; to see heads, we had to rise.

Hearing something, I looked out and saw [Jesús] Montané.[3] I didn't recognize him, because he was without his glasses. Imagine, skinny and bearded! But Melba knew at once that it was Montané. I didn't want to believe it, and I didn't want to disappoint Melba, but looking hard, I saw him groping to find his way, like a man who couldn't see without his glasses, and thought: "It *is* Montané." And I told Melba so.

I don't know how many days had passed in that cell, eight or nine. Waiting for Fidel, we had lost hope that anyone would come. We thought everyone had been captured in the mountains, because by now we were sure they had not all died at Moncada. And days and days went by and no one came. We knew that what they had was not enough to make any real resistance; they could have held out for a day at

---

[3] Havana accountant and friend of Abel Santamaría; director of tourism under the revolutionary government in 1961.

most. We were convinced that they would not appear.

Then, when Montané arrived, it made us see that Fidel, too, might come. From that moment, we didn't move from the grating for a minute.

Neither of us breathed a word. We were so firmly glued to the grating that even when they came to bring us meals I was unaware of it. I pushed my dish out full and they emptied it and refilled it, or maybe they only pushed it back through the bars with the same stuff in it. It meant nothing to me; my mind was not working on that level. I simply waited.

Then one day we heard footsteps, and voices louder and more excited than usual. Something big was happening. But if something big—what could it be?

Then in a moment I saw some hands in motion, some fingers. I don't know how I knew, but—they were Fidel's. "Melba, it's Fidel!" I said. She looked harder, searched harder. Then she grabbed me and embraced me, crying, "Yeyé,[4] it *is* Fidel!"

[4]Yeyé: pet name for Haydée.

It seemed impossible, but she showed me how to look so that I could see his face. And it *was* Fidel.

We had been neither dead nor alive. Now we broke free of that thing—you must experience it to know it—that is neither life nor death. And from that moment the question whether we lived or died no longer mattered. Fidel was alive. Moncada lived!

VI

"I WAS A PRISONER,
SHACKLED AND MANACLED,
AND I FELT STRONGER AND
FREER THAN THOSE WHO
WERE GOING TO JUDGE ME"

The mass trial of 122 accused insurrectionists and conspirators opened on September 21 in the Palace of Justice in Santiago. Many of those before the court had no knowledge of Moncada whatever. Among them were former officials of the administration of ousted President Prío Socarrás. In seizing power in 1952, Batista said he acted in order to prevent Prío from retaining the presidency by an armed coup. Now, still seeking to justify the golpe of March 10, Batista accused Prío as the secret author of the Moncada plot. Thus the Santiago trial was a political show, with a foregone conclusion.

THE TRIAL had been expected for some time, but there was so much concern among us for Fidel's life that the two things ran together.

I remember being taken by bus through the town to the court. In those moments, I began to love Santiago the way I loved the tiny little town where I was born; because Santiago, too, had been able to see that we, the accused, were good, not evil.

The town wanted to see our trial. And I remember how, when I faced the court, I saw its cowardice. And at that moment I stopped believing in judges; I ceased to believe in law, in lawyers, in magistrates. And I began to believe in men.

Some of the judges who were present then may be revolutionaries today: if they are, they are my comrades. But that does not mean that I should not express what I felt at the time.

Being brought to trial, I detested the robe called justice. Today it still exists here, and I still cannot tolerate it.

I believed so strongly in men and so little in judges that I could not imagine receiving justice at the hands of those people in their robes and caps. I had never seen anything so ridiculous! I found it all absurd. I was scornful of the whole proceeding. And I felt so strong!

I was a prisoner, shackled and manacled, and I felt stronger and freer than those in the robes of justice who were going to judge me.

I had no wish to speak. There was no need to talk to my companions, and the people were not present. What *was* present was repression, and those who called themselves "interpreters of the law."

For a moment I had the desire to say: "I have no statement to make to you. Some day I will make a declaration before the people; but you, you give me the impression of being scarecrows. Justice is not dispensed in a cap nor does it wear black rags: it is clothed in dignity and truth; one dies in its defense."

And I was certain that no one of those judges was ready to die, or even to listen. But then I thought again: "Since they don't want to hear, they will." And so I stated and affirmed and declared and told them:

"I left the civil hospital with twenty-five comrades, and now there are two of us.

ПЛПЛПЛПЛ ПЛ ПЛ ПЛ ПЛ ПЛ ПЛ ПЛ ПЛ ПЛ ПЛ ПЛ ПЛ Г

Twenty-three are missing. You symbols of justice, tell me where they are."[1]

And they made no reply.

At that moment I felt about them the way I
felt about [Colonel Alberto del Río] Chaviano.[2]
It may be unjust, but I must speak the truth: I
go on detesting that so-called justice and I stand
against it; I ask judges nothing about justice. I
believe in analysis and in conscience, not in justice out of a book. For a human being is not a
receptacle that you do this or that to; a human

---

[1]As previously noted, Haydée had the number wrong:
there were twenty-one in the group, including Abel Santamaría. Two survived.

[2]Chaviano was the commander of the Santiago zone of
operations and the officer principally responsible, under
direct orders from Batista, for the post-Moncada massacre in which, as Fidel related: "Before dawn groups of
men—already deformed by torture—were taken from
[Moncada], their hands tied and their mouths taped.
They were taken to Siboney, La Maya, Songo, and other
places to be killed in solitary fields. Later these deeds
were recorded as deaths in combat with the army. This
they did during several days, and very few prisoners of all
those who were arrested survived. Many were forced to
dig their own graves."

being is a life. And ten thousand books can never teach me anything about justice. I apply justice by discussion, by argument, not by applying mechanically what books tell me or the law tells me, even if it is a law of the Revolution. For although the Revolution makes no mistakes, the man who wrote the law in question may be mistaken.

I have faith in human beings, and not in pieces of paper.

VII

☆

**"IT MEANT LIVING AGAIN,
FIGHTING AGAIN,
ACTION, LIFE!"**

*Haydée and Melba Hernandez were found guilty of
sedition and sentenced to six months' imprisonment.
They were confined before and for a while after the
trial, with the others, in the prison at Puerto Boniato,
outside of Santiago, then transferred to the penitentiary at Guanajay to serve out their terms.*

IT WAS A QUIET TERM, or else I felt very
quiet. In Santiago there really was a fighting
spirit, because we had an objective. There was
the trial, the preparation for the trial . . . so
those two months at Boniato were magnificent,
marvelous, fighting tyranny. But in Guanajay,

for me, it was a time of . . . lying on a bed and reading. There was nothing else to do. We were alone, Melba and I; there were no other political prisoners.

I never regarded prison as a painful experience. In Boniato it was great because it was very militant. It was to seek justice, to fight for Fidel's life and for our dead; it was to carry on the struggle. It was not that we believed in bones and dust, but to strike a blow at despotism, to keep our dead from being snatched away. From Boniato we directed the job that had to be done in Santa Efigenia [cemetery] and in other places so that those bodies would not vanish into thin air.

So then, Boniato was good, militant, whereas Guanajay was terrible because of the quiet and the lack of anything to do, of not being able to do anything. On the other hand, departure was a tremendous shock. It was to see the marvelous sun again, the palms—to see them, and to know that others would never see them again. It was to confront reality head on, and to despair, wondering how we would channel our lives, who would give us work, how to earn money in order to fight.

By then my family had a firm understanding of our struggle. But of course they wanted me to come home—we lived in the sugar *central*[1] called Constancia, today known as Central Abel Santamaría—fearing that if I returned to Havana I would only be arrested again. We had never lost touch; there were my parents, my brothers and sisters, relatives, friends. Still, for me it was maddening to think that, no longer confined in a prison, I would be confined in what was, in effect, a tiny little town; I mean town in the sense of friendships, fond neighbors. I had been born there, and so they spent their lives watching over me, and that was the maddening part.

In any event, we kept on going—they had wanted to take Melba, too—and came to Havana and lived in Melba's house. It was a difficult time; Melba's father felt dreadfully unsafe

---

[1] A Cuban *central* is, in effect, a small village, including not merely the mill where the cane is ground, pressed and converted into sugar, but the canefields, stables, machine shops, outbuildings, school and homes of sometimes as many as a thousand year-round employees and their dependents.

with us in the house. Again in touch with others keeping up the struggle, doing something every minute, we were worse than the plague. In spite of it, we stayed on, and carried on the fight until at last Fidel and the others left the Isle of Pines.

It meant living again, fighting again, action, life!

VIII

☆

"WE WERE GETTING TO KNOW
HISTORY WILL ABSOLVE ME"

Fidel Castro's secret trial took place on October 16, ten days after the mass trial of his followers concluded. It was held, not in the Palace of Justice, but in an anteroom of the provincial hospital, while more than a hundred soldiers guarded the corridors. His defense, consuming more than five hours, centered on the illegitimacy of the Batista regime. He was charged with rebellion against the constitutional powers of the state. How could he be guilty, he argued, when those very powers had been usurped by the dictator, and had ceased to have any legitimate force? His arguments and summation, written in his cell and smuggled out a scrap at a time, to be published by the underground under the title History Will Absolve Me, *provided the broad social document that stands as the manifesto of the Cuban Revolution.*

WE WERE GETTING TO KNOW Fidel's declaration, *History Will Absolve Me,* through ways and means that we found effective in prison, little by little. When Melba and I left Guanajay, we got in touch with his sister Lidia, and this is how we got it out.[1] Sometimes we received the wrong pages—not the ones that belonged together, but the last or the first, and we had to coordinate them and put them in place.

Fidel had told us to get out one hundred thousand copies. "The man has gone out of his mind in prison," we said. "How are we going to get out one hundred thousand copies when we can't even produce five hundred?" So we wrote to him, saying that it was impossible.

[1]In the Sierra in 1957, Fidel told me that he had written "a very interesting little book" called *La Historia Me Absolverá,* using onion juice or sometimes lime juice as invisible ink between the lines of ordinary letters. Heated, the writing became visible. It had been difficult, he said, because he could only work when the sun entered his cell at the right angle for seeing the glistening juice.— R.T.

"It is not a matter of money," we told him. "We have a press, we've collected the money; it is just that one hundred thousand is a lot of copies."

His answer was: "Well, and what is the difference between getting out twenty-five and getting out a hundred thousand?"

Then I started to analyze: "We're all set up; let's give him as many as we can."

Later he wrote and said: "Look, I'm in prison and I can see more than you can. Now then, one hundred thousand means the same amount of work as twenty-five. It is all in the preparation, the setting up that you have to do. Once it is done, you can print twenty-five in ten minutes and a hundred thousand in twenty-four hours. Just get out as many as you can. Take the first five hundred off the press immediately and put them in a safe place. And so with the next five hundred, and the next, and the next."

So we printed ten thousand, not a hundred thousand, because when we had reached ten thousand we saw that we might be discovered and lose a press and a lot of helpful people. We told Fidel, and he answered: "That is why I asked you to get out a hundred thousand. If I had told you to print five hundred, you would have aimed for five hundred, and you might never have printed the ten thousand."

Once we had the copies, we didn't know how to distribute them. A comrade, Gustavo Ameijeiras, said: "Look, if you can get hold of forty-five pesos, I can get a jalopy."

We raised the forty-five pesos and bought the jalopy. Then he said, "Listen, if you can get me two pesos, we'll put in some gasoline."

We found two pesos and put in the gasoline and loaded the car with the whole crate of *History Will Absolve Me,* and Gustavo drove to Oriente.

When he returned I asked him how he had managed it. "Oh, it was simple," he said. "Wherever I went I came across a friend—not a revolutionary friend like the ones you have here who don't know what they are, whether revolutionary or not, but the ordinary ones going about their business. The friend would ask me: 'Have you settled down now? Are you through with all that nonsense?'

" 'Yes, of course, *chico,*' I would say. 'Of course. I'm in business here.' "

And he would make up a business; I think he said life insurance. "But, imagine," he would tell his friend. "I have things to do in Santa Clara and I haven't a penny, and the gasoline tank . . ."

And so his friends would take him out for *café con leche* and lend him a little something. So that is how he got to Santa Clara, and that is how he reached Oriente and distributed *History Will Absolve Me*.

It all seems so easy now.

IX

☆

"TO LET CUBA DIE
WAS TO KEEP TALKING,
TO KEEP SAYING THAT
THE CONDITIONS FOR CHANGE
DID NOT EXIST"

WE COME NOW to political questions.

I am asked what I can say about my brother Abel's political ideas and plans. Abel died in his first action, which is to say, very early. He was not one of those who were to die later, during the landing of the *Granma* from Mexico, or still later at Playa Girón,[1] as happened; for many of those who went to Moncada died afterwards in the Sierra Maestra or at Girón.

Abel was a studious boy, and although he had ideas that we called, at the time, leftist, he always found an answer in [José] Martí.[2]

[1]Playa Girón: Scene of the CIA-sponsored invasion of April 1961, generally referred to in the American press as the Bay of Pigs.

[2]José Martí: Cuban poet, philosopher, and national hero, who died in the War of Liberation against Spain.

He studied Martí, read Martí, for fourteen years, and through Martí went looking for other things that no longer had to do with his own country or with Latin America. He wanted to learn something about other continents, so he read Lenin and Marx, as much as could be read when there was not enough money to buy books or even the time to find them.

I believe—but here one has to guess a little—that in those days Abel was laying plans for changing Cuba. He was convinced that Cuba must not be permitted to die. And to let Cuba die was to keep talking, to keep saying that the conditions for change did not exist. Because to make things happen one had to create the conditions. Not once but on several occasions he told me: "We will shape the conditions and we will go on shaping them, or others will. What we cannot continue to tolerate is to say that in Cuba nothing is worth the trouble, that you must live as best you can, that Cubans are miserable creatures and do not deserve any better."

He used to say, "All Cubans deserve everything, and it doesn't matter if we run risks, if it makes Cubans realize that they deserve to have us take action for them and stay in it."

That is, Abel decided that he had to act to

show the people that there was still some dignity in men, even if there was no dignity in those who shaped the system. He wanted people to be aware of it.

I don't know whether he proposed to live or die. He always talked as though he were going to live for many years; he talked about what he was going to see and what was going to happen. I don't know whether he thought he would actually see it, or imagined what others would see.

He had an exceptionally truthful nature; he was extraordinarily kind and high-principled and infinitely sensitive. At every moment he did what needed to be done. And he felt that he had to do what he did.

His political belief at that time was Cuba—this present Cuba. I don't know what he called his convictions, because I never asked him, but I do know that it was this Cuba he loved. Often when we were passing through Camp Columbia,[3] he would say: "After this is turned into a

---

[3]Campamento Columbia: army headquarters in Havana and principal barracks area of the Batista regime.

school and there are thousands of children here instead of thousands of soldiers, all will go well; it can't go badly." Today Columbia—Ciudad Libertad—is full of thousands of children instead of soldiers.

X

☆

"I AM NOT GOING TO SAY
THAT WE WENT TO MONCADA
TO MAKE A SOCIALIST
REVOLUTION"

I AM NOT GOING TO SAY that we went to Moncada to make a socialist revolution. It is not so. We went there with the idea of making a change, so that better men might govern and so that men would not steal, but not exactly to make that change. Once there, I felt the change to be urgent. But if we went there without intending to make a radical change, it was to make *some* change, and it was to tell our people, our country: "There are those who die for the flag," for the same flag we have today, for the flag we love today.

We knew little about profound changes; we could not determine what the change would be when it came; but we knew that Fidel would determine what it would be like, and that we would make it what our people wanted it to be.

And we knew that our flag would continue to be our flag.

We went to Moncada as disciples of Martí. Today we are Marxists, but we have not abandoned Martí, for there is no contradiction. We went there with the ideas of Martí, and today we still have those ideas, as well as the ideas of Lenin, Marx, and Bolívar: we are continuing Bolívar's revolution, Ché Guevara's revolution, too, with the leadership of Martí, with the doctrines of Marx. We still follow Bolívar and strive for the continent that he tried to unite.

How did we arrive at the Marxist-Leninist conviction?

Again I must speak personally.

Nothing that exists, and that is proposed to us in life as a necessity, is painful. We proposed the necessity, and the changeover was normal, like a person growing, like a child who is born and doesn't know how to walk. First he stands, then walks, then runs, then is ten years old, fifteen, twenty.

That is the way it was presented to me. First, the changeover had to be total. Then it had to be ours, absolutely ours. Since necessity is not painful—well, there it is.

I continued performing necessary tasks, carrying out duties—we all did—and gradually we saw the need of creating a new man, a new consciousness.

How was it to be done? Well, by changing the system, and letting the new system change the man.

There is need for a doctrine to change men, and it was easy to find it. What I did not want was a false doctrine; I have never accepted a false doctrine, either before or after Moncada.

And my idea of being a Communist does not mean only joining a party; it means having an attitude toward life.

XI

"IT WAS BECAUSE
FIDEL WAS FIDEL,
FIDEL,
FIDEL!"

NOW AND THEN someone will ask me about Fidel. Has he changed?

The truth is, I have always found it irritating to hear people say, "How Fidel has changed!" as if it were something remarkable.

Fidel has changed like anyone else. If he had stayed as he was at Moncada, he would be abnormal. *I* have changed; even I. We all have. And if I've changed—I who am an ant beside an elephant—imagine how much the elephant must have changed!

Someone of Fidel's generation, someone who knew him at the University, will say: "Now I'm solidly behind Fidel, because he has changed a lot." And my reply is: "The truth is, chico, that the one who has changed is *you*. Because three days after meeting Fidel, I had no doubts. I wasn't with Fidel at the University, I never knew him the way you did, but three days after he started coming to my house it was no longer Abel that I followed, but Fidel. And only someone of tremendous personality and tremendous character can do that. Because I tell you that for me Abel was not just anyone. And yet, within three days . . ."

University students tell me, almost proudly: "I'm taking Fidel's course, you know. But look, you see what's happening? Because look how Fidel has changed!"

And I say, "What an imbecile you are! You tell me how *you* have changed, and lucky for you that you have, because Fidel has not."

There is no contradiction. Fidel is the same, but with a whole series of things added that are working slow changes in him. What doesn't change, doesn't exist. And with Fidel, just imagine the change!

As to the transformation that came over me from the moment I accepted his leadership, it was not only because Abel accepted it, but because Fidel was Fidel, Fidel, Fidel!

XII

☆

**"AFTER MONCADA
WE SAW THAT THE PROBLEM WAS
NOT TO CHANGE A MAN,
BUT A SYSTEM"**

LIKE ALL CUBANS, we who went to Moncada have lived through many things, some
greater, some smaller, all with very deep feeling. And I have wondered why, if we survived
Moncada and the Sierra Maestra and before the
Sierra the underground, if we survived the bat-
tles of 1959, and later Girón, enormous things,
why then was Moncada different from all the
others?

At times I've said that the explanation came
to me, very clearly, when my son Abel was
born. When my son was born there were difficult moments, such moments as any woman
goes through when she is bearing a child. The
pain was terrible, pain enough to tear out one's
insides, yet there was also the strength to keep

from crying, or screaming, or cursing. And why? Because a child was coming.

That was Moncada. In spite of the pain, the feeling of being lost, the sorrow there, greater than any other, I believe we kept our serenity because of what we knew was to come from it all. I believe it is only because of the coming of something great that one can stand such grief. The birth of the child we await cannot be greeted with tears or screams.

I speak of the first child, the first action. One may not love the first any more than the second or the last, but the first is different: we are not prepared for it, we don't know whether we will be able to stand the pain.

All of this gives us a different feeling toward the second and the third and those to follow. Understanding it showed me clearly what Moncada had been. It was not the action we loved best; it was not the greatest, either; but it was the first: we had not known how we would face it, how much of it we could endure. Perhaps we went prepared to see some dying, prepared to leave there some who should have lived for many more years. But the unexpected also happens: we were not prepared to stay alive, we who survived Moncada.

Until those moments, I had known that terrible things could exist; I had been told what things men were capable of doing. But I had faith in men; it made me incapable of imagining how a society could turn men into monsters.

The shock of seeing it happen totally changed our lives. When we talk in ordinary conversation of any small event, we who were at Moncada, we say, "This happened before . . ." or, "This happened after . . ." And *before* and *after* always mean before Moncada, after Moncada.

The transformation after Moncada was total. We were still the same people, capable of the same passion, but the transformation was great—so great that if we had not made a series of plans for the future it would have been difficult to go on living, or, at least, to go on being normal.

After Moncada, we saw clearly that the problem was not to change a man—this is to speak of Batista: it was to change a system. But it becomes clear, too, that if we had not gone there to change the man, perhaps the system would not have changed.

In prison I thought of how much we could continue to do, and the will power it would take to do it. I will always remember—it is as fresh in my mind as it was the first day—when Abel said to us: "After this, it will be harder to live than to die, so you must be braver than we are, because we are going to die—and you, Melba and Haydée, must live, must be stronger than we are. You will find that a harder thing to do."

Today it is all different. Today we go off to fight with the full support of the nation, the full support of those we love. At Moncada we were beginning a battle without the people's support—or if they were behind us, we had no way of knowing. We were fighting without the support of our own families. We were considered fools in those moments when we brought pain to those we loved, and we were sorry for the pain we caused them, and for their lack of understanding. We were sorry we grieved them so deeply, and sad to think that our children might remember it as the mad act of fools.

This is not to say that we had no faith in our people or in our children. Rather, it is to say that acts that endure, when they do, stand as the acts of a few unyielding men. Moncada achieves greatness through the courage of those who die and those who live. Moncada would have been nothing without the courage of those who died there and without the courage of those who lived.

We had that fear: what will they think of us, at least during these first years? Our pain was intense, because we were going to give everything and we were going to gain everything.

It is not to say that going to Moncada was something heroic: it was a privilege. Many women, given the chance to be near an Abel, a Boris, or a Fidel—and so many others that to name them would make an endless list—would have gone, had they been so privileged.

At the same time, it was difficult. What girl of eighteen or twenty is afraid to pick up a gun today? Today the fear is of what her son might say if she did not. Today's concern is when my son asks his father: "Why don't *you* wear olive green?"[1]

In the past a child might say: "My father didn't love me. He went away and left me, without any food, without a house to live in." Today the child asks: "Are you in the front lines, did you go into the field, did you go to Girón, are you a militiaman?"

---

[1] That is, the army uniform.

There was sorrow before Moncada, the sorrow of hearing José Luís Tassende[2] say: "I always loved my daughter. I didn't abandon her. I came here because I loved her so much." He was not sure that his daughter would ever understand, so he would repeat it again and again.

Those bound for Moncada were leaving their children without fathers, food, or homes to live in, and all they sought was a little dignity—something not quickly found, nor easily.

The years work transformations in our inner selves. I often think, "But why did we suffer so much?" It was because today everything has changed. If we went off to fight now, I wouldn't have to say what Pepe Luís said; I would know that my children had a mother, I would be sure of their having a school and teachers and a university to study in; they would have as much as Pepe Luís's daughter has today. But Pepe Luís doesn't know it.

[2]Killed at Moncada.

XIII

☆

"I NEVER CONSIDERED THE ATTACK ON MONCADA A FAILURE"

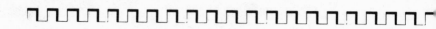

I OFTEN ASK MYSELF, why is it hard for me to talk about things that were easy to do? When it is something like Moncada, I think that if I haven't actually forgotten, I may have tried to forget. And then I realize that it is not so.

Rather, it is that so many thoughts and memories come to mind so quickly that it becomes impossible to express them. A thousand thoughts come tumbling head over heels, and I can only talk about one at a time.

Something happens with dates. What is loved lives, but dates make me remember, bringing with them a flood of feeling. The twenty-sixth of July, 1953. What I remember is that on that day we lost a group of heroes whom I knew and loved.

They live in history and in the minds of us all.

With every passing year, the event becomes greater, because the Revolution grows greater. The more this nation accomplishes, the greater Moncada will be. And so every day it will be harder to talk about Moncada.

There is this to say: when I am asked how I felt after I knew that the attack on Moncada had failed, I reply, "You may not believe this is the truth, but I tell you sincerely, it is: I *never* considered the attack on Moncada a failure."

AFTERWORD

☆

In search of better opportunities, Abel moved to Havana, and within a short time Haydée joined him. Although Abel found a well-paying position, and they lived in a comfortable apartment in a central part of the city, both were disturbed by the situation in the country. Those were years of the embezzlement of public funds, the growth of gangsterism, of division within the labor movement, of submission of the country to imperialist intrigues: Prío Socarrás governed the abused neo-colonial Republic.

Abel and Haydée were both attracted by the implacable denunciation of the political reality made by Eduardo Chibas and by his motto "Shame on money." They soon became active members of the Orthodox Youth and met with other young workers who, like themselves, without abandoning a joyful approach to life, believed that the country required immediate and profound change. Even after the death of Chibas in 1951, they believed that this change could be brought about by an election victory of the Orthodox Party, a foregone conclusion in the elections that were to be held within several months.

The Batista coup d'état on March 10, 1953, destroyed these hopes. Abel and Haydée were among the first to take concrete measures against the coup. Together with their comrades, they published an underground mimeographed newspaper, *Son los Mismos (They Are the Same Ones),* and carried out an intense agitation campaign. One afternoon, Abel returned home with a new comrade—Fidel Castro.

When the time and place for the initial battle were determined and it became necessary for Fidel and Abel to select the participants, two women were among them: Haydée and the young lawyer Melba Hernández.

The target: Moncada garrison. There are numerous accounts of the battle. Throughout these accounts, the figure of Haydée is always present.

Once when she was caring for casualties in the civil hospital, she saw a soldier lying on the ground. She decided to help in spite of the rifle fire from both sides. She approached a doctor who had remained in the hospital and tried to force him to accompany her. The doctor refused. He didn't want to risk himself unnecessarily in the midst of the firing. In addition, were they not the ones who had wounded the soldier? Why worry about him now? Haydée heatedly explained to the doctor that they had not come to murder for pleasure, that there were laws of war, that it was only humane to help the enemy. The doctor was not to be convinced, but the argument attracted another doctor, who immediately offered to help Haydée.

They crawled out to where the soldier was lying. The doctor examined him. "Señorita," he told Haydée, "this man is dead. We can return." Haydée did not meet the doctor again until her trial, when she had to respond to the accusation that she had prevented a physician from caring for a wounded soldier who was bleeding to death. When called upon to testify, the doctor who had gone out with Haydée under fire told the court that the accusation was true.

But the first doctor, the one who had refused

to risk himself, energetically refuted the charge, and testified that just the contrary had oc-curared, that Haydée had sought him out to at-tend the soldier, and that he had refused to ac-company her because of fear.

Which of the two is good, Haydée was later asked—the doctor who risked himself under fire but weakened in front of the judges, or the one who fell apart under combat but later defied reprisals?

Haydée's answer: "The one who remained with the Revolution."

The confrontation between good and evil reached terrible extremes in those moments. When Abel understood that the barracks had not been taken and that there was no longer any fighting, he ordered his men to continue shoot-ing from the hospital for almost an hour in or-der to give survivors from the attack on the bar-racks time to escape.

This decision was fatal. Haydée would later extract a decisive lesson from the experience. At that moment, she feverishly moved from one part of the hospital to another, disguising her comrades as patients when their ammunition was exhausted. She bandaged her brother Abel's face as if he suffered from an eye illness.

All in vain. Troops entered the hospital and, led by an informer, arrested the attackers one after the other. The soldiers began to beat Abel, Gómez Garcia, and Dr. Mario Muñoz, among others, as soon as they left the hospital. Muñoz was killed on the spot.

Haydée still relives those days in all their vivid detail. Nothing can be added to Fidel's words in his court address, *History Will Absolve Me:*

With a bloody human eye in his hand, a sergeant with several men appeared in the jail where the comrades Melba Hernández and Haydée Santamaría were being held; the sergeant turned to Haydée, showed her the eye and said to both of them: "This is your brother's; if you don't tell us what he wouldn't tell us, we will tear out the other." She, who loved her brother above all else, answered them with dignity: "If you tore out one of his eyes and he said nothing, even less will I say anything." Later they returned and burned her arms with lighted cigarettes, until finally, they said to the young Haydée Santamaría: "You no longer have a fiancé, because we have killed him also." And very serenely she answered them once again: "He is not dead, for to die for your country is to live."

In those moments, Haydée did not know whether Fidel himself was alive. She was alone with Melba confronting the horror, forced to discover strength within herself. She would draw out this strength as if through some extraordinary childbirth she would give birth to herself. She would no longer be the same as before, but, nevertheless, she became herself in a singular manner.

Moncada was not only a military battle; it was also a legal battle and, above all, a political battle. As a military battle—followed by an atrocious slaughter—Moncada signified a defeat for the attackers, but in the other two spheres it was a triumph. It has been rightly pointed out that the trial of the attackers was of enormous importance because it converted them into implacable and courageous prosecutors of the regime.

Haydée played a fundamental role. Survivor of the massacre, witness to the cruelty that had torn from her those who were most beloved to her, she gave damning testimony. Martha Rogas, who attended the trial as a journalist, has reported that when the court clerk called out, "Haydée Santamaría Cuadrado!"

. . . the announcement of this name caused intense emotion in the courtroom, because she was considered by all the members of the tribunal to be the principal witness for the defense after Fidel; and for (Col. Alberto del Rio) Chaviano she constituted a very real danger, for Haydée had been an eyewitness to the worst infamies committed by the guards on the 26th of July.

"Haydée, dressed in black, serious, very serious, without being tense," Martha wrote afterwards, "told the judges serenely and firmly the whole truth about the atrocities that followed the Moncada attack."

Haydée and Melba were sentenced to seven months in the prison of Guanajay. The prison term was hard. Even before sentence, the two women had been placed among common criminals, who, it was hoped, would harm them. But the convicts were more considerate than the criminals who held power. After the formidable presentation of all the comrades at the trial, the insurrectionary process had taken on even larger dimensions, and Melba and Haydée had new tasks assigned to them when they would leave prison. Much reading filled their hours in the "university of revolutionaries" which was the prison. While Fidel was doing the same in his cell on the Isle of Pines, Haydée read and made notes on the complete works of Martí. The volumes, with marginal notes in her handwriting, are still preserved.

In 1954 Haydée and Melba were free. Their first mission was the clandestine circulation of *Mensje al Cuba que Sufre (Message to Suffering Cuba)*, a manifesto in which Fidel explains to the people how his brothers were savagely massacred. And soon the most important mission: the editing and distribution of *La Historia Me Absolvera*, which Fidel had reconstructed and smuggled out of his prison sheet by sheet. Thousands of copies were read throughout the country and abroad.

The next year, Fidel, Raúl, Juan Almeida, Ramiro Valdes and the other survivors were freed.

"It was living again," Haydée said later. A dramatic photograph preserves the meeting: Haydée embraces Fidel, her head on his chest.

With Fidel free, the revolutionary process could not be stopped. It now had a name which at the same time was its watchword: *The 26th of July Movement;* Haydée became one of the members of the National Direction. When Fidel went to Mexico to organize the *Granma* expedition, Haydée went underground, with the name María.

Towards the end of 1956, while awaiting the arrival of the *Granma*, Haydée traveled to Santiago. On November 30, she was among the organizers of an uprising in that city that preceded the *Granma* landing by a few days. Cornered in a large house as the shooting was coming to an end, Haydée recalled the lesson of the hospital. They could not remain to be captured; they had to escape by any means. They succeeded. With her were new comrades in the movement, Frank País *(David)*, Vilma Espín *(Deborah)*, and a restless lawyer she had met in the underground and had married several months before, Armando Hart—he was called *Jacinto*.

The life of the married couple was filled with danger. Hart, who had made a spectacular escape from the Havana Court of Justice was sought by the police as Haydée was. In the cities they were able to see each other for only a few days between missions. They also met in the Sierra Maestra, where Haydée found new and close comrades, among them one with whom

ππππππππππππππππππππ

she exchanged repartee and for whom she found medicine for his asthma: Ché Guevara.

On one of the occasions when Hart was leaving the Sierra Maestra to carry out a mission, he was arrested and sent to the Isle of Pines. Shortly afterwards, Haydée was sent abroad to fulfill various tasks for the movement.

When the Revolution came to power, on January 1, 1959, Hart left prison and became Minister of Education. Haydée was named director of the Casa de las Americas.

She finally had a home. Two children were born: Abel Enrique and Celia María.

She also became a member of the National Direction of the United Party of the Socialist Revolution, when the revolutionary organizations joined together. And on October 3, 1975, when the Central Committee of the Communist Party of Cuba was created, her name was there. (Armando Hart became a member of the Political Bureau.)

Haydée has explained with absolute clarity the ideological evolution that brought the attackers against the Moncada to embrace the Marxist–Leninist doctrine when the revolutionary process took on a higher degree of radicalization.

There [Haydée once said] we were becoming followers of Martí. Today we are Marxists and we
haven't ceased being followers of Martí, because
there is no contradiction in that. We went to the
Moncada with the ideas of Lenin, with the ideas of
Marx, with the ideas of Bolivar, with the revolution
of Ché; with the direction of Martí, with the direction of Marx and Bolivar, with the continent that
Bolivar wished to unite. . . .

It is not strange that the Revolution should
place important responsibilities on the passion-
ate follower of Martí, the fraternal comrade of
Ché—he wrote his last and unforgettable letter
to her. In 1967 she presided over the conference
of the Latin American Organization for Solidar-
ity. In addition she has been uninterruptedly the
head of Casa de las Americas from the time of
its foundation in 1959; under her direction, Casa
carries out an intense task of affirmation, defense and circulation of the values of what Martí
called "our America."

On this woman who was with Fidel in the
darkest moments of the Revolution, a woman

overflowing with inexhaustible energy and with laughter and flashing anger and a sorrow that is like a wound; on this woman who has preserved the clear eyes of girlhood, Commander-in-Chief Fidel Castro placed the first Order of Ana Betancourt on November 29, 1974. He must surely have recalled that day in Santiago, twenty years earlier, when he declared: "Never before has the name of Cuban womanhood been raised to such a high place of honor and dignity."

Roberto Fernandez Retamar

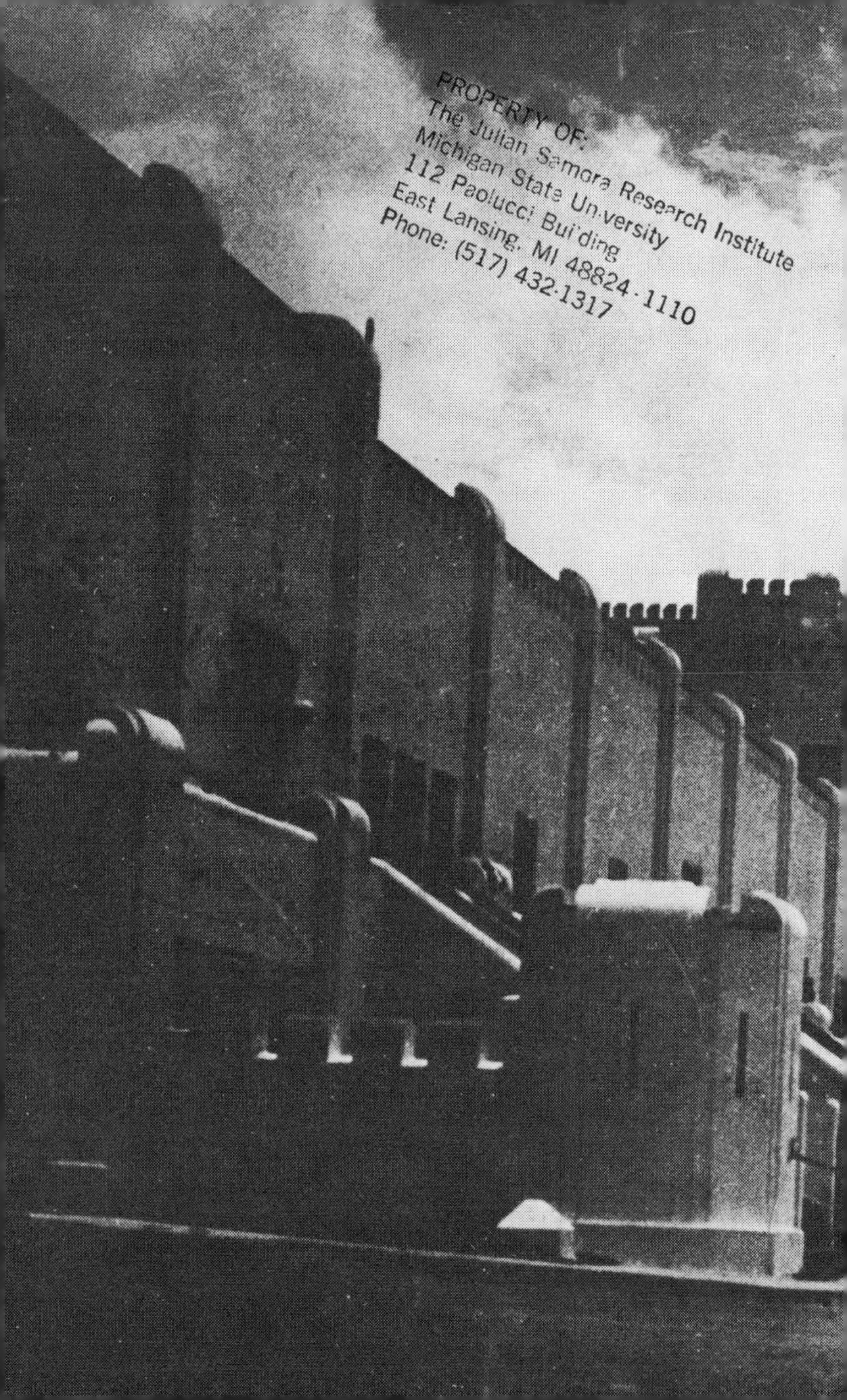